We're Off to See the Lizard

Author
Barbara Brenner

Illustrator
Shelley Dieterichs

♠ Raintree Editions

We're Off to See the Lizard

Text copyright © 1977, Barbara Brenner

Illustration copyright © 1977, Raintree Publishers Limited

All rights reserved. No part of this book may be reproduced or utilized in any form or by any means, electronic or mechanical, including photocopying, recording, or by any information storage and retrieval system, without permission in writing from the Publisher. Inquiries should be addressed to Raintree Publishers Limited, 205 West Highland Avenue, Milwaukee, Wisconsin 53203.

1 2 3 4 5 6 7 8 9 0   81 80 79 78 77

Library of Congress Number: 76-10350
Printed in the United States of America.

Published by   Raintree Editions
         A Division of Raintree Publishers Limited
         Milwaukee, Wisconsin 53203

Distributed by Childrens Press
        1224 West Van Buren Street
        Chicago, Illinois 60607

Library of Congress Cataloging in Publication Data

Brenner, Barbara.
 We're off to see the lizard.

 SUMMARY: Two children discover a green anole in their backyard and learn about its habits and life cycle.
 1. Anolis carolinensis — Juvenile literature.
[1. Lizards] I. Title.
QL666.L2B83 598.1 76-10350
ISBN 0-8172-0150-5 lib. bdg.

To Jennifer

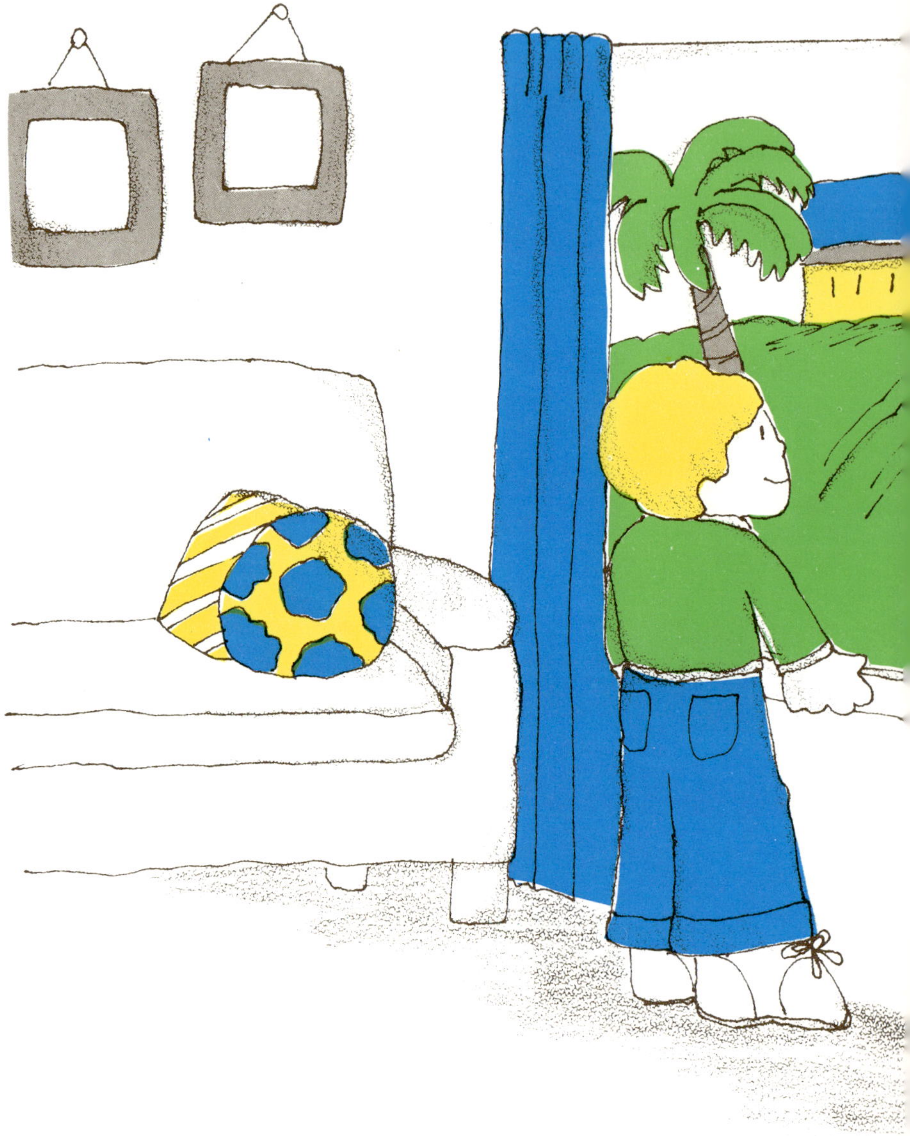

Harry and Annie had just moved
to Florida. Harry was sitting
inside their new house.
He was thinking.
"I hope we are going to like
it here," Harry said out loud.

Just then Annie called to him
from the garden.
"Harry! Come out here. I've
found the strangest thing!"
"What kind of thing?" Harry
called back.
"Well — it's green."
"Like a plant?"
"No. Like an animal. It has
four legs and a tail. Come look!"

Harry came. And there it was —
a little green animal with
a long, skinny tail.
It was sitting on a plant.

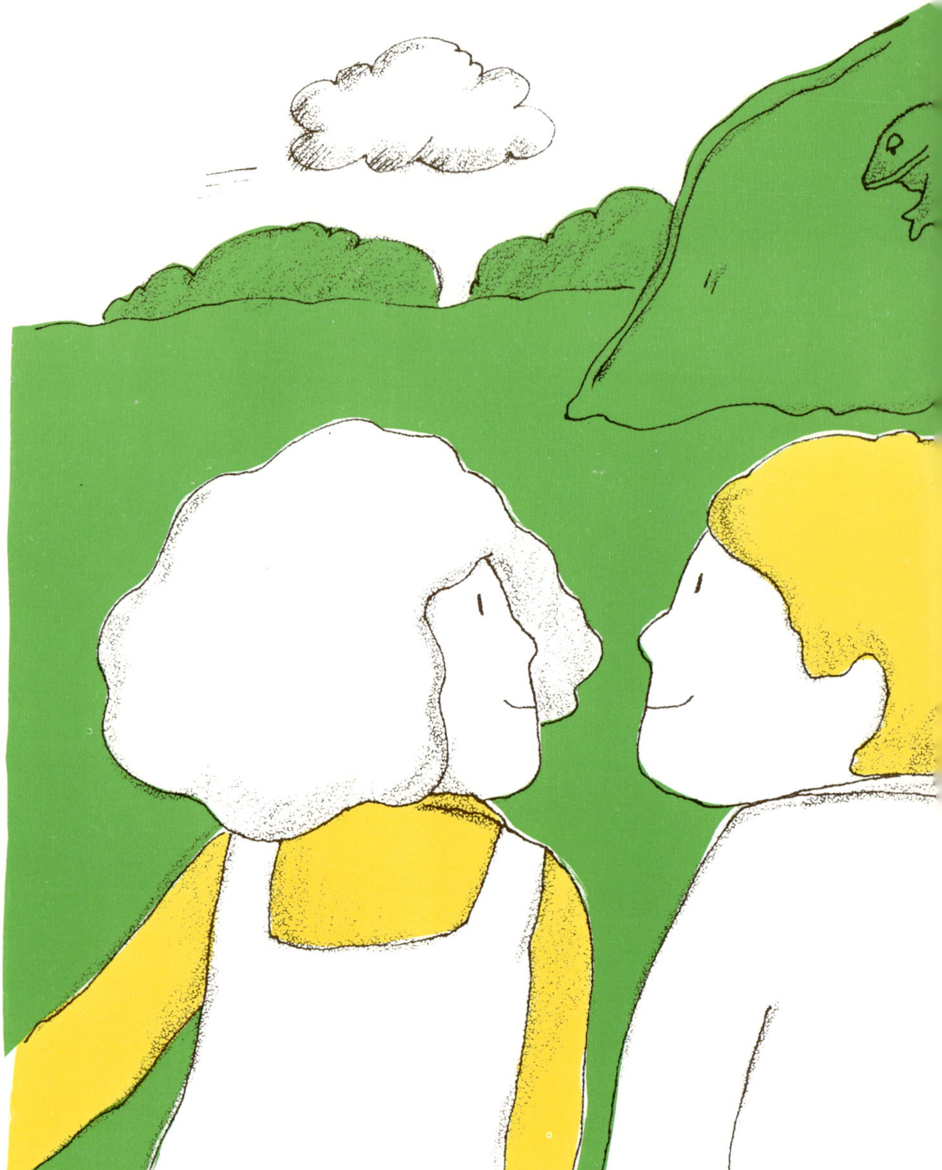

"Annie!" cried Harry. "You've
found a little dinosaur!"
"Harry," said Annie, "there
are no more dinosaurs, remember?"
"There could be *one* more,"
said Harry. "This could be it."
"No," said Annie. "I'll tell you
what this is. It's a dragon."
"Annie," said Harry, "dragons are
make-believe animals, remember?
Besides, who ever heard of a
six-inch dragon?"
"Maybe it's a *baby*," said Annie.

"Hi, baby dragon," she called.
"Hi, yourself," said a voice.
A girl stepped from behind a palm tree. "I'm Meg," she said. "I live next door."
"I'm Annie," said Annie. "We're twins. We just moved in."
"I'm Harry," said Harry, "and this is our baby dinosaur."
"*Dragon*," said Annie.
"**Dinosaur!**" Harry shouted.
"*Lizard*," said the girl named Meg. "That's what I came to tell you. That green thing is a lizard."

13

14

"Why does a lizard look so much like a dinosaur?" Harry asked.
"Because lizards and dinosaurs are relatives," Meg told him.
"Like twins?" asked Harry.
"More like cousins," Meg said. "They both had the same lizard ancestor millions of years ago."
"But the dinosaurs all died, right?" Annie asked.
"Right," Meg agreed. "There are no more dinosaurs. But there are over 3,000 kinds of lizards."

"What kind is this one?" Harry
wanted to know.
"Some people call it a
chameleon," Meg told him.
"But its real name is *Green Anole*.
And I have three of them
at my house."
"Then let's go to your house,"
said Harry.
"Follow me!" said Meg.
The three children went over the
garden wall to Meg's house.

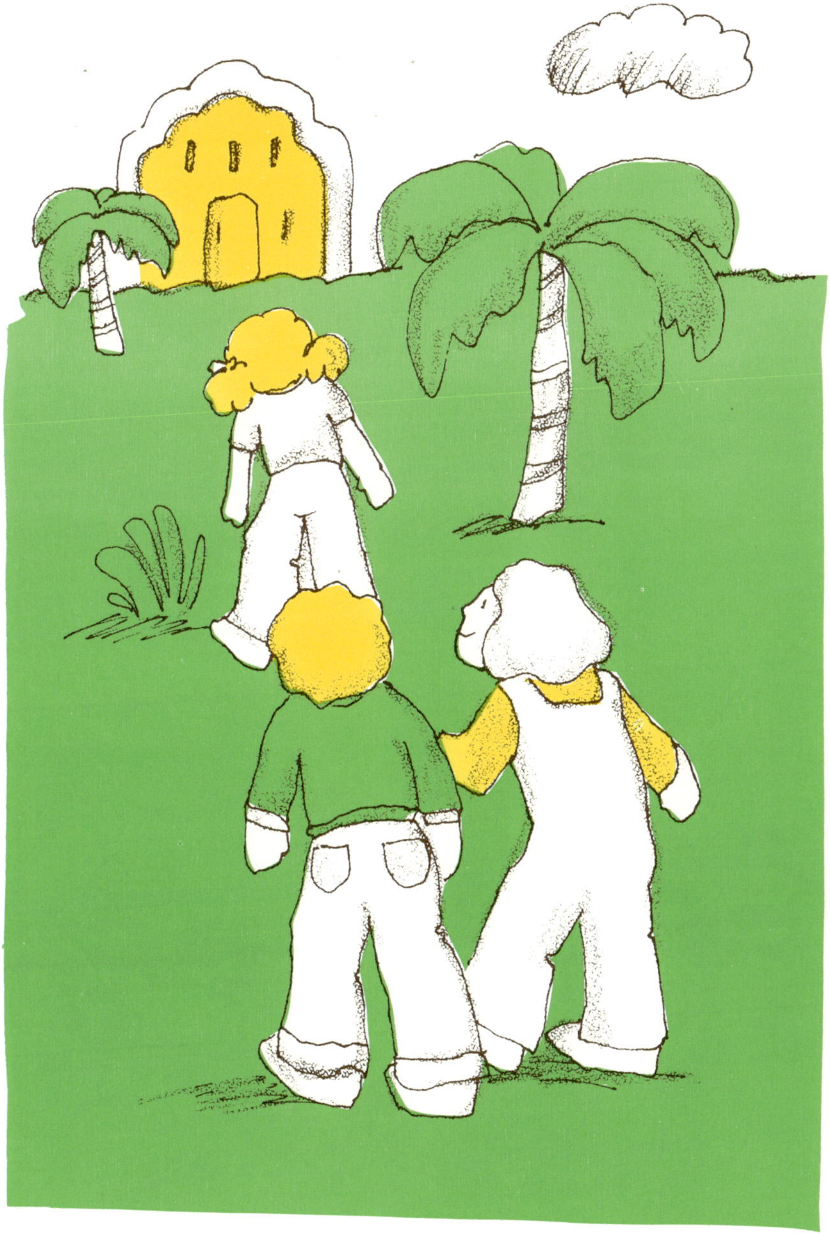

The anoles were in Meg's room.
They were in a glass tank with
sand at the bottom and plants
for the anoles to climb on.
There were rocks
for them to hide under
and water for them to drink.

"Hey," cried Annie. "Your anoles are brown. Ours were green." "Sometimes mine are green," said Meg. "They change color."

19

"Animals can't change color," said Annie. "That's silly."
"Anoles can. Other kinds of lizards can too."
"I'll bet they change color to hide," Harry guessed. "If an anole is on something green, it turns green, right?"
"Wrong," said Meg. "Heat makes them do it — and light. Sometimes when they fight, they change color. When a male wins a fight, he turns green. If he loses, he turns brown."

21

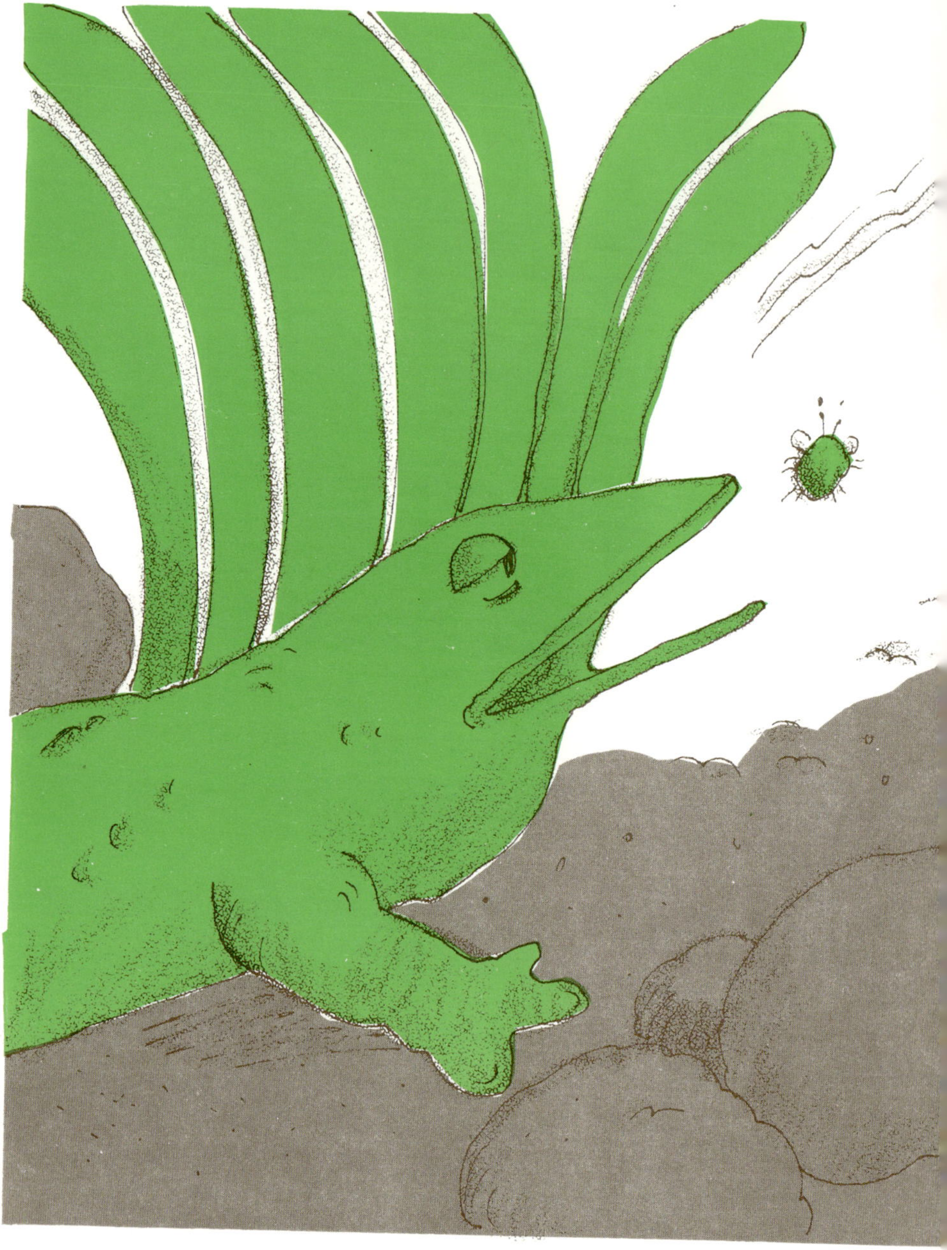

"Meg, have you seen anoles change color?" Annie asked.
"Yes, I have. Lots of times."
"Then I guess they do it."
There were some bugs in the tank. One of Meg's anoles snapped at a bug and ate it.
"Is that what anoles eat? Bugs?" Annie asked.
"Bugs and worms," Meg told her. "A bug or worm is like hamburger to a Green Anole."
"Bugburger!" said Harry.
"Wormburger!" said Annie.

"Sometimes anoles eat fruit," Meg added.
"Fruitburger!" the twins cried.
Annie put her face close to the tank. "I see that anoles have teeth," she said, "and big jaws!"
"And look at the claws on their feet!" said Harry.
"They use them for climbing," said Meg. "And they also have special pads on their toes. See how they run up the side of the glass tank without slipping!"

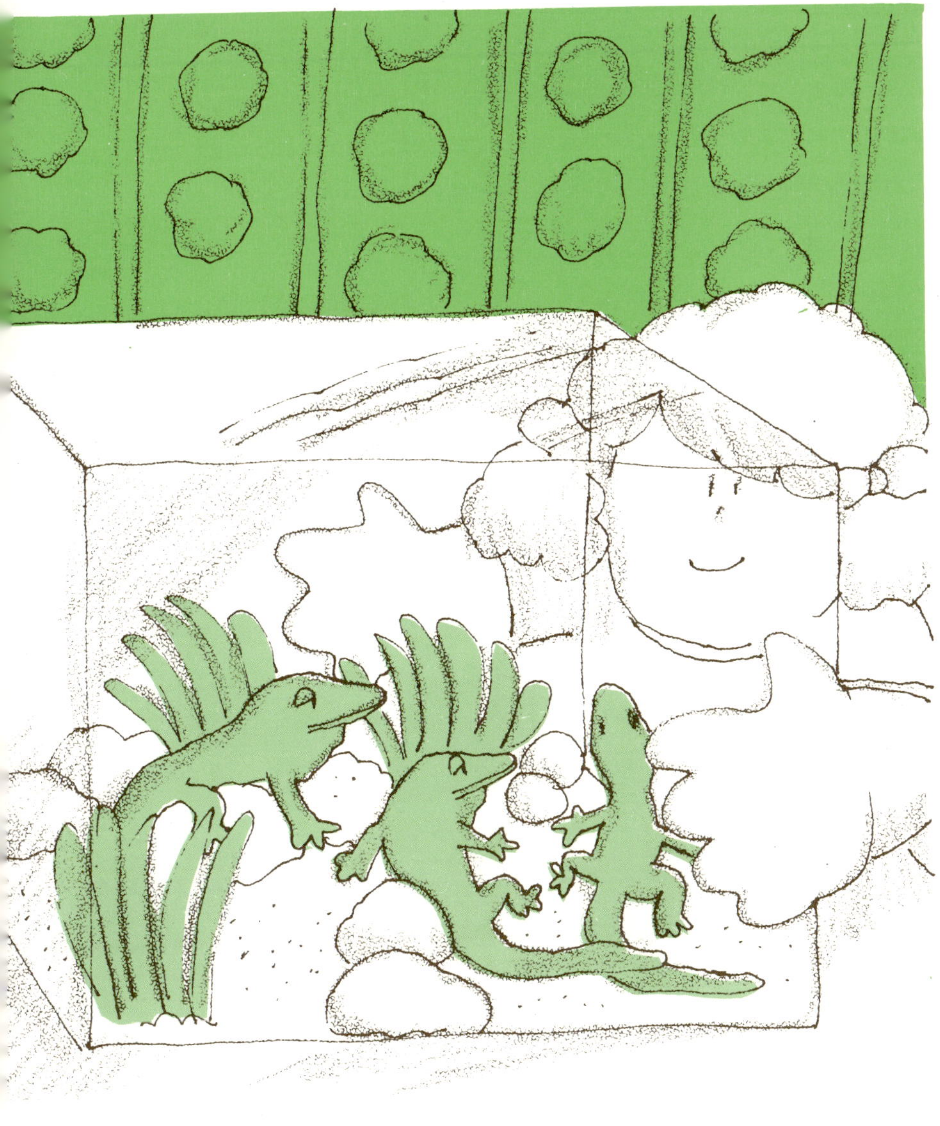

One of the anoles began to
bob its head up and down.
The skin under its chin fanned
out. It was bright red.
"Meg," Harry asked, "what's that
red skin under the anole's chin?"
"That's his *dewlap*," Meg said.
"What's it for?"
"It's to make him look big and
scary. He fans it out when he
wants to scare another male or
show off for a female."

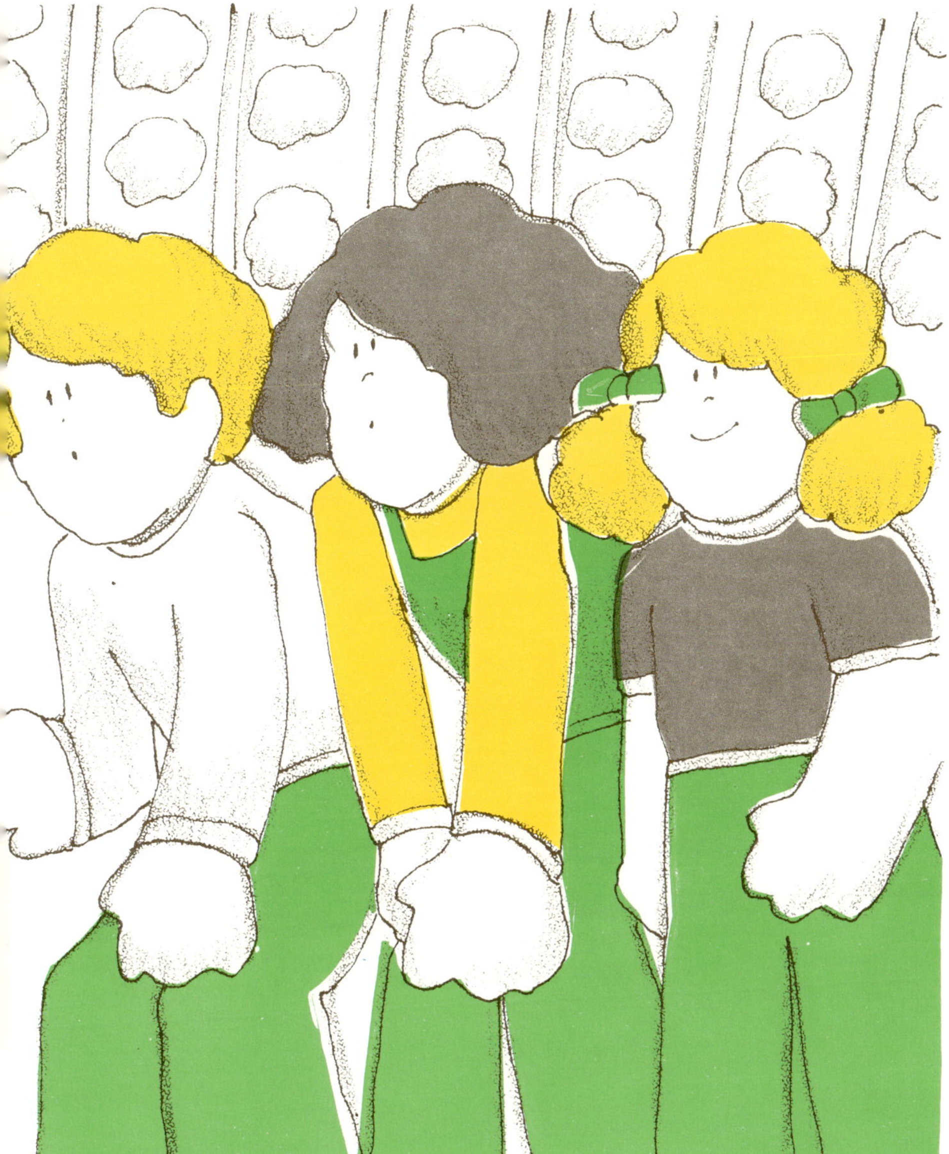

"Do female anoles have dewlaps?"
Annie wanted to know.
"No," said Meg. "But they lay
eggs. Lots of them.
After mating, the female
digs a hole with her snout.
She lays one or two eggs
in it and covers them with sand.
Two days later she lays another
egg in another hole. She lays
eggs all spring and summer.
They hatch in about ten weeks.
By fall there are baby anoles
all over the place."

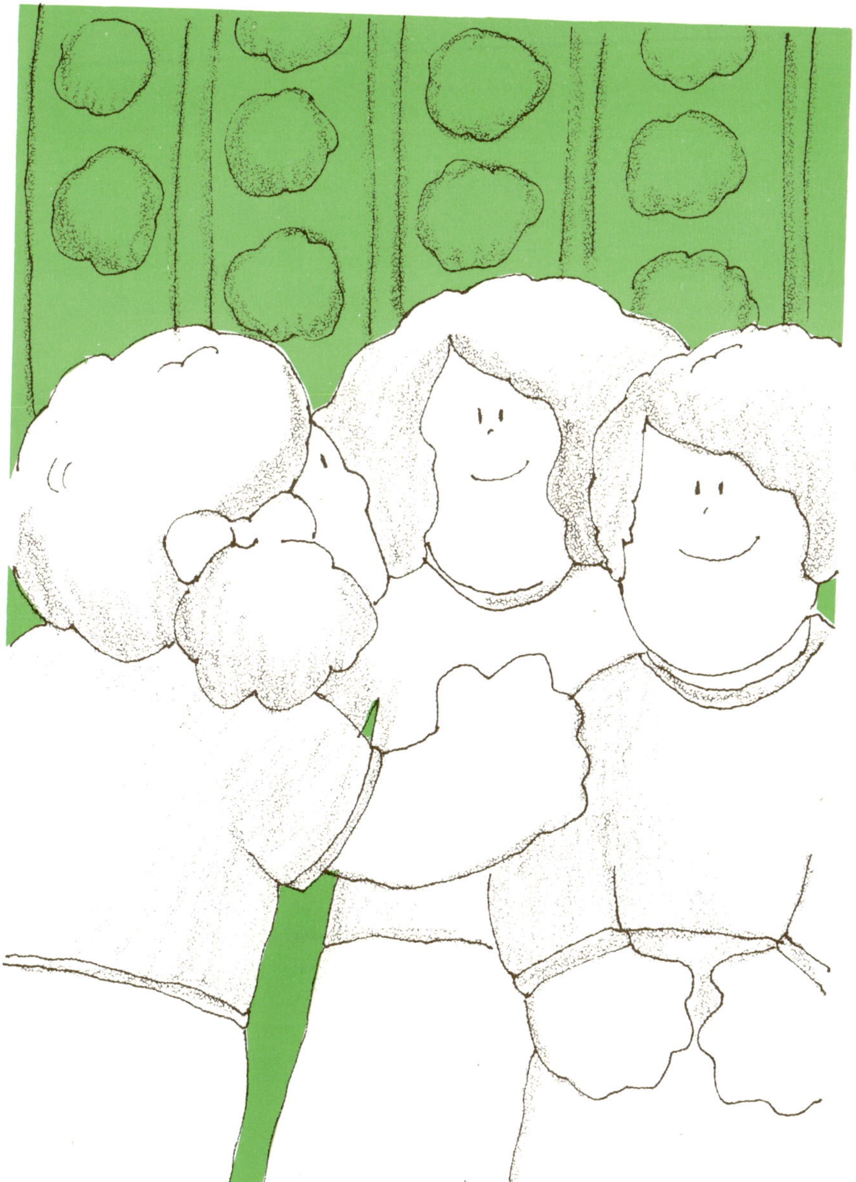

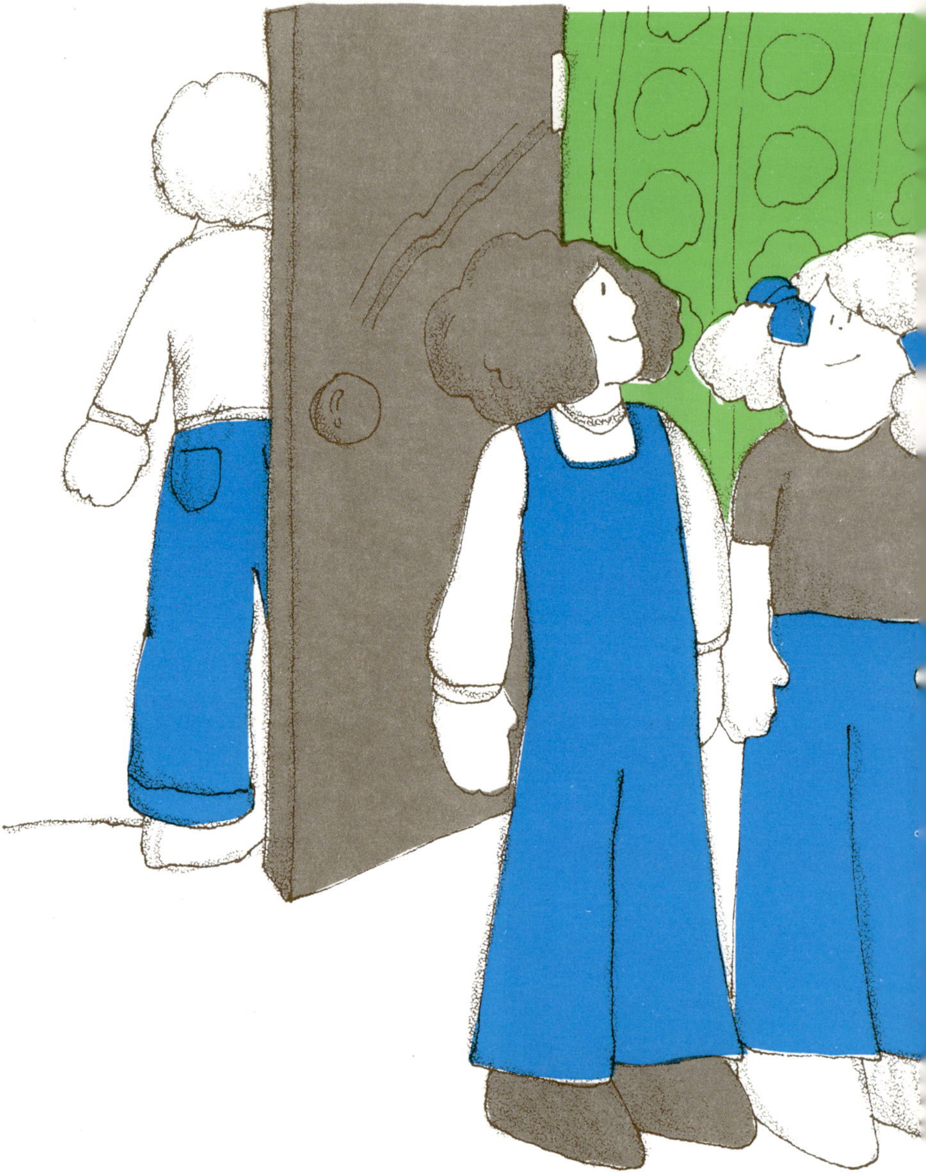

"I think having babies is even better than having a dewlap," said Annie.
"I really like these anoles. I want to hold one," said Harry.
"Not one of my anoles!" Meg said sharply. "There's a special way to catch and hold a lizard. And if you don't know how . . ."
But Harry didn't hear her.
He had run off to catch an anole in his garden.

A little later Harry called,
"Annie! Come here! Hurry!"
Annie ran next door.
"What's the matter?" she asked.
"I caught the anole," Harry said.
"Good for you."
"Yes. But *bad* for the anole.

Something happened. The anole's tail came off right in my hand!"
"Wha-a-a-t?"
Harry held out his hand.
There was the lizard's tail — still wiggling.

"Yecch! Where's the rest of it?" asked Annie.
"It ran up the palm tree."
"We had better get Meg," Annie decided. "Meg! Come on over!"
Meg looked over the wall.
"What's up?" she asked.
"An anole is up," said Annie.
"It's up in the palm tree."
Meg nodded. "They do that. They run up into trees."

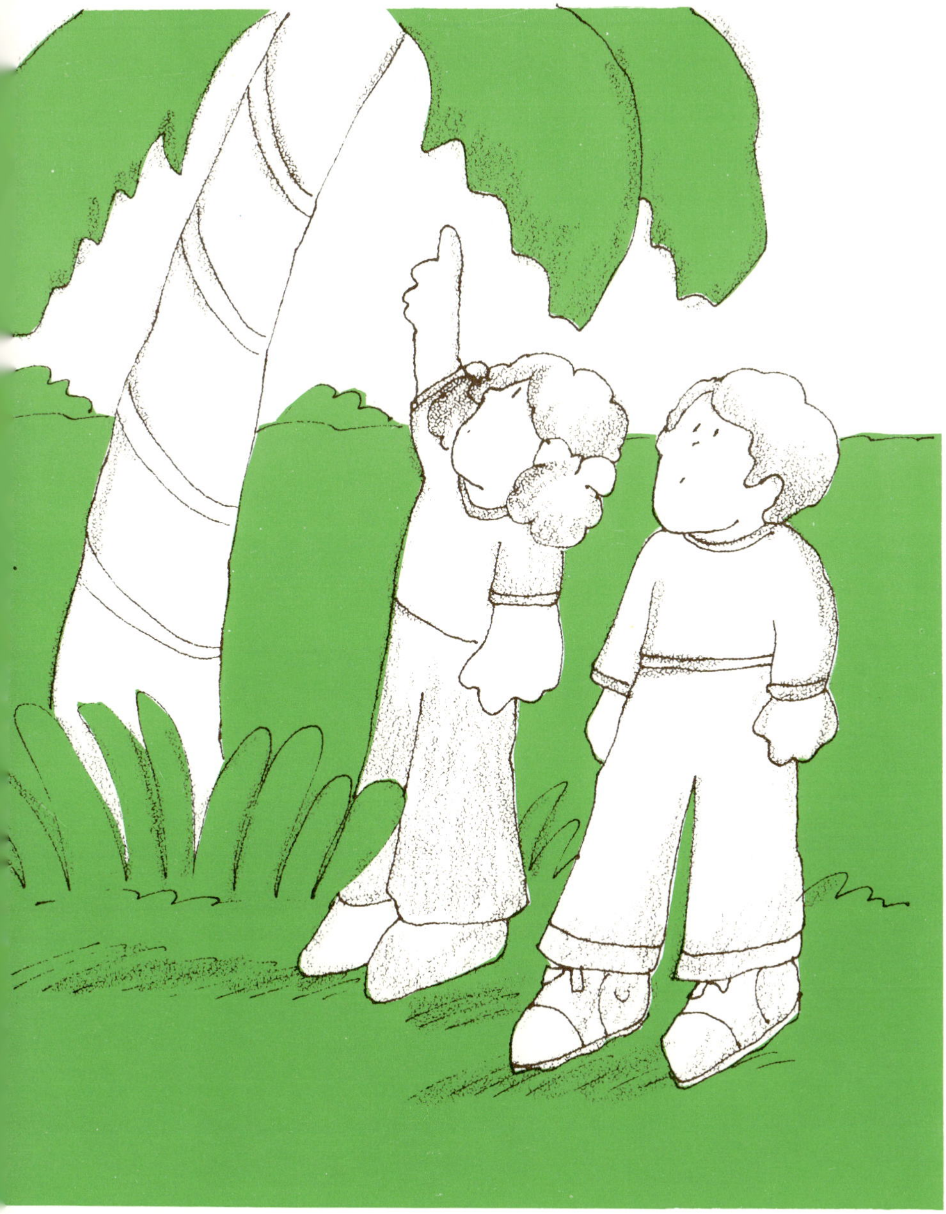

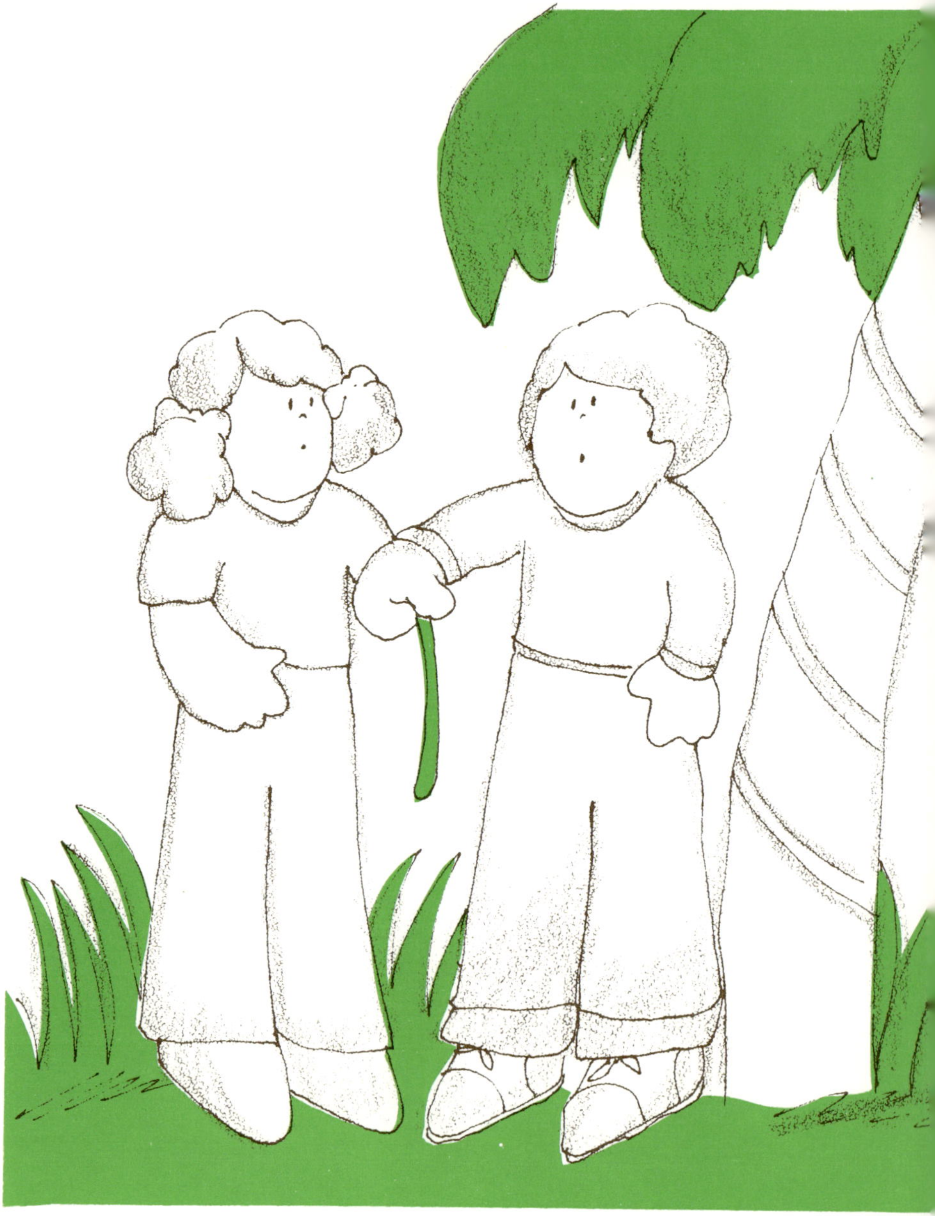

"Yes, but the *tail* of this one is down here!" Harry showed Meg the tail. It was *still* wiggling.
"Oh, Harry," said Meg. "I knew there would be trouble if you caught a lizard. Now you've made it lose its tail!"
"I didn't *pull* it," said Harry.
"I know. But sometimes the tail comes off if you grab the lizard.

That's how the animal gets away."
"Gets away from what?" asked Harry.
"From a bird that wants to eat it. Or from a snake."
"Or from a *Harry*," giggled Annie.
"The anole will grow a new tail," Meg told them. "But it will take a long time."
"I'm sorry I did it," said Harry.

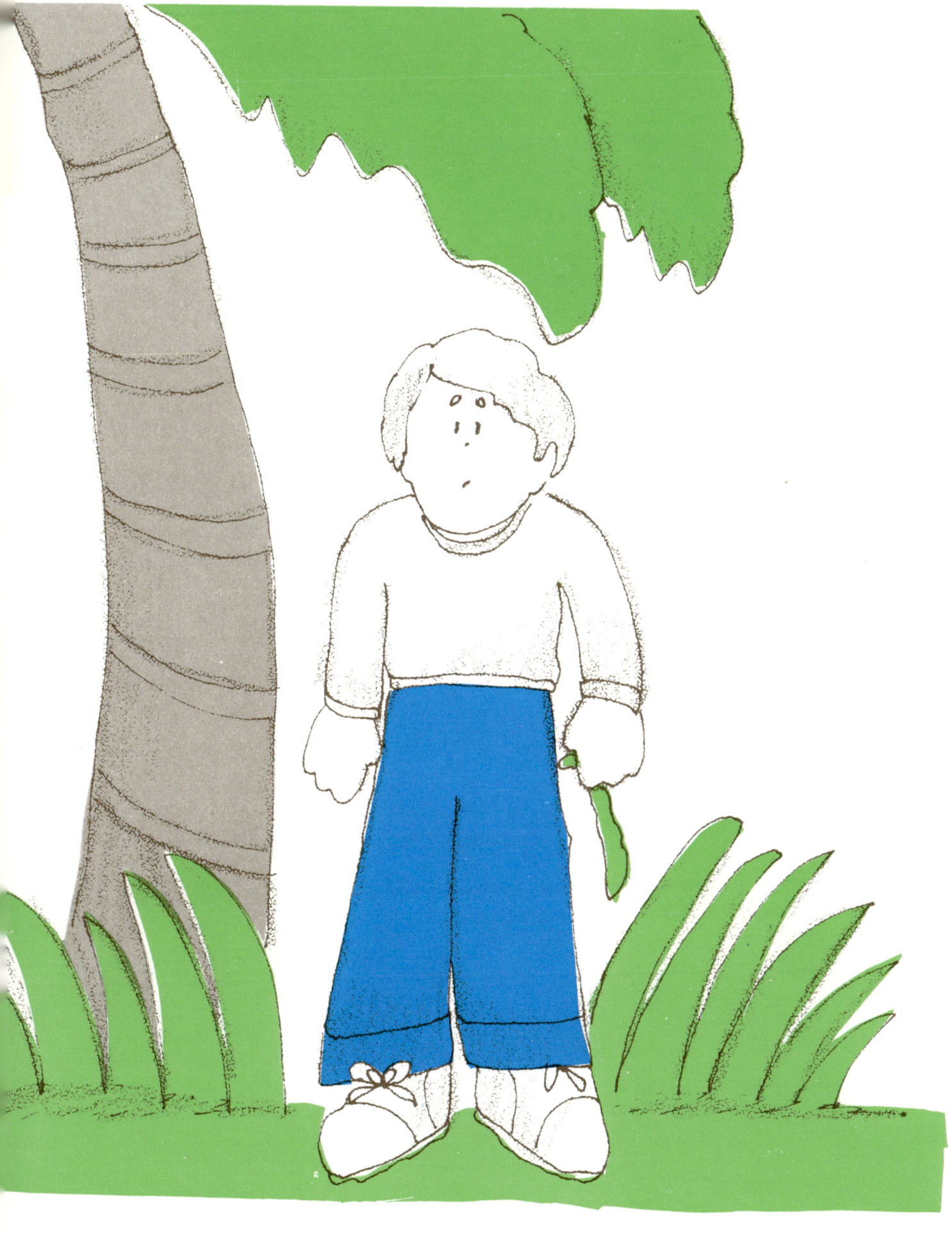

"Never mind," Meg said. "Let's go back to my house. I'll show you how to hold an anole so the tail won't come off."
"Will you show me too?" Annie asked her.
Meg promised to show them both.
"Now watch me," said Meg.
"First I catch the lizard. You have to move fast. I put my hand around it and hold its neck between my fingers. Easy — like this. And I stay away from the tail!"

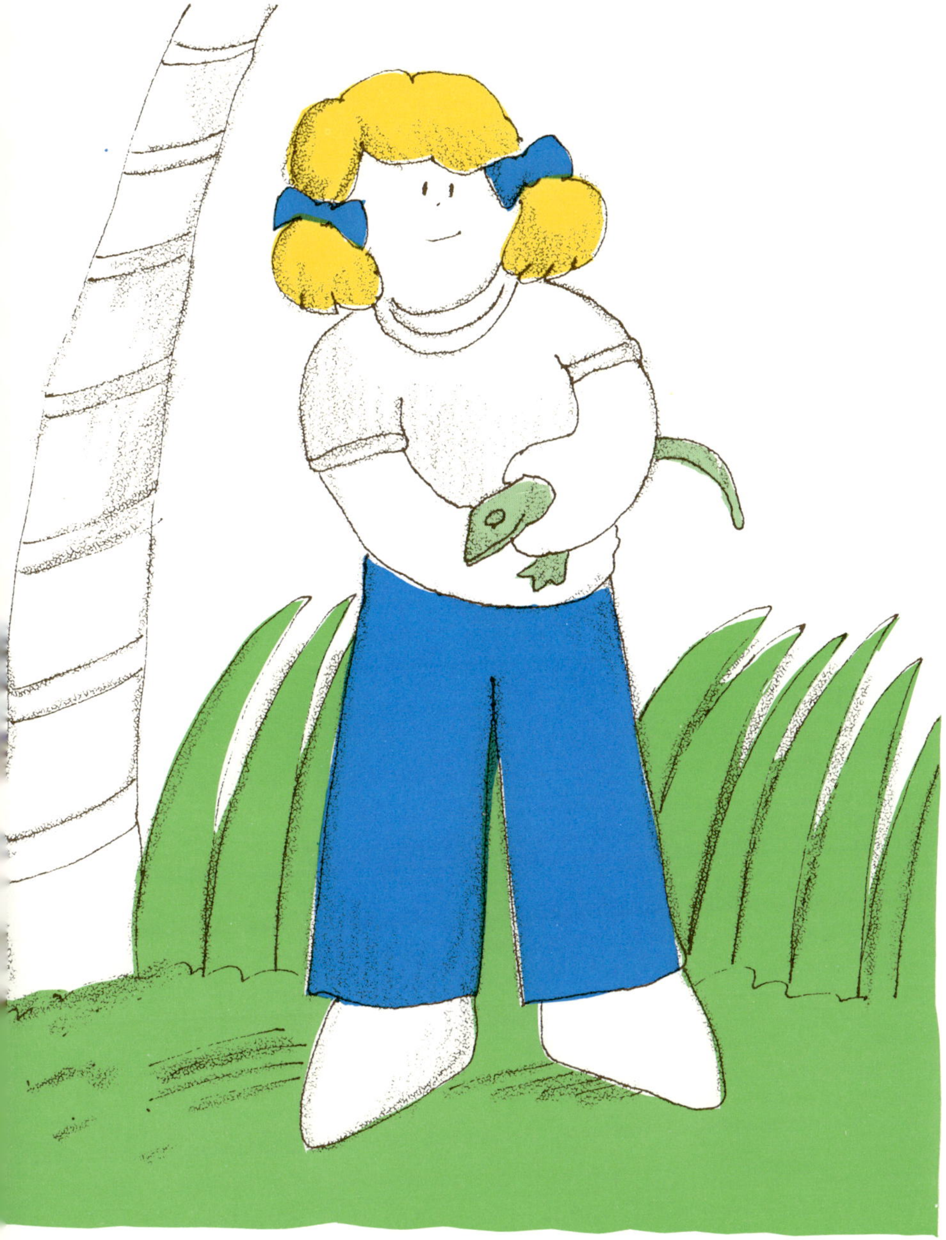

"Oh, let me try," said Annie.
"Me too," said Harry.
Each of them caught an anole and held it. Then they both put them back in the tank.
Annie sighed.

"I wish I had Green Anoles in a tank in my room," she said.
"I'll help you catch some," said Meg. "And I have an old tank you can use."
Now Harry sighed.
"I wish I could see all the lizards in the world," he said.

Meg laughed.
"You can't see all of them.
But I know a place where you
can see a lot of them."
"Where?" asked Harry.
"At the zoo. They have lizards
there from all over the world.
There's one that's poisonous and
one that can glide through the
air. And one so big it looks
just like a real dragon!"

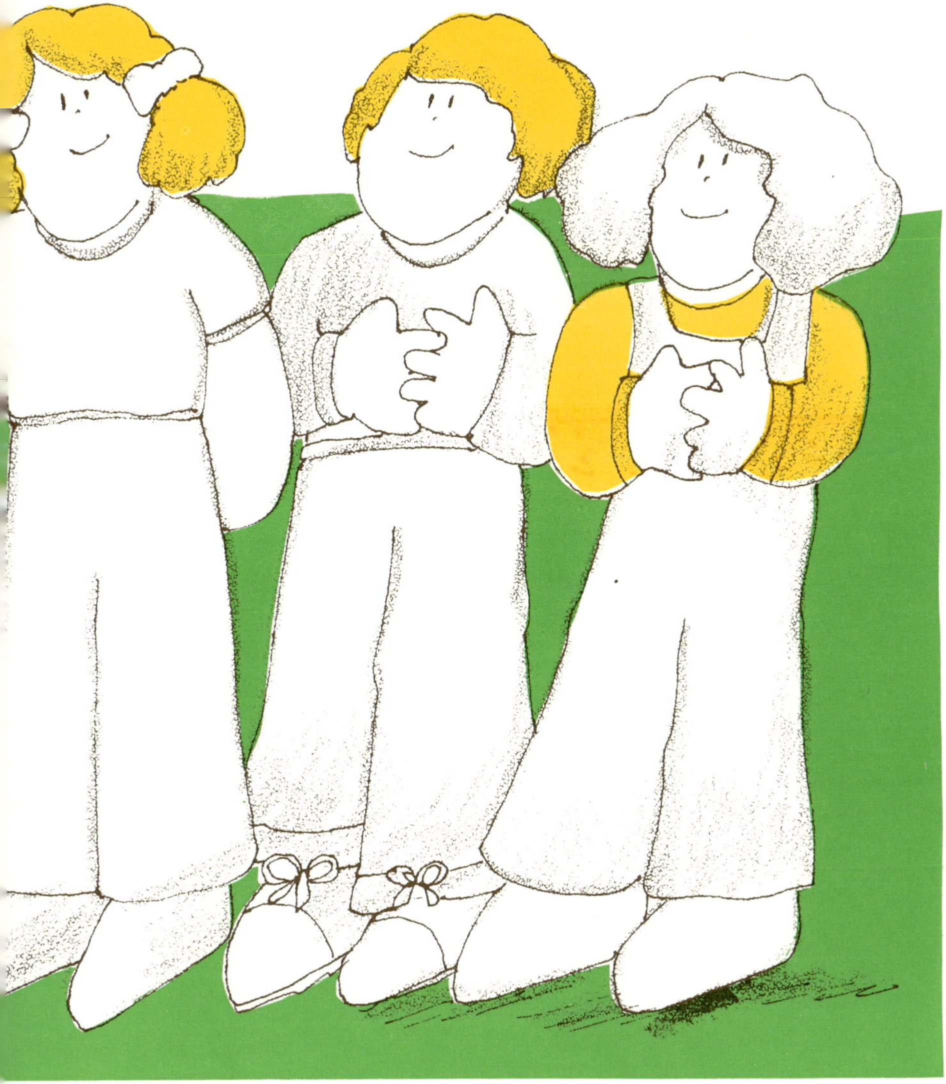

"Can we go to the zoo?"
"Sure," said Meg.
"When?" asked Harry.
Meg said, "How about right now?"
"Right now is perfect," said Harry.
"I'll go tell Mom where we're going."

"Hooray!" cried Annie. "We're off to see the lizard!"
"The lizard," sang Harry, "the wonderful, wonderful lizard! Oh, Annie, I think we're going to like it here!"